Contents

Family favourites

From naughty to nice this delicious assortment
will bring out the child in all of us.

Orange poppy seed cupcakes

MAKES 15

40 g (1½ oz/¼ cup) poppy seeds,
plus extra to sprinkle
125 ml (4 fl oz/½ cup) warm milk
150 g (5½ oz) unsalted butter, softened
3 teaspoons finely grated orange zest
170 g (6 oz/¾ cup) caster (superfine) sugar
2 eggs
185 g (6½ oz/1½ cups) self-raising flour, sifted

Citrus icing (frosting)
250 g (9 oz) unsalted butter, softened
375 g (13 oz/3 cups) icing (confectioners')
sugar, sifted
3 teaspoons finely grated orange zest

Preheat the oven to 180°C (350°F/Gas 4). Line
15 standard muffin holes with paper cases.

Combine the poppy seeds and milk in a bowl and set
aside for at least 15 minutes.

Place the butter, orange zest, caster sugar, eggs and
flour in a large bowl. Add the poppy seed mixture and
beat with electric beaters on low speed until
combined. Increase to a medium speed and beat for
3 minutes, or until the mixture is thick and pale.

Divide the mixture evenly among the cases. Bake for
15 minutes, or until a skewer comes out clean when
inserted into the centre of a cake. Transfer onto a wire
rack to cool.

To make the citrus icing, place the butter, icing sugar
and zest in a large bowl and beat with electric beaters
until light and fluffy. Spread the icing over the cakes
and sprinkle with the extra poppy seeds.

Plum crumble patty cakes

Preheat the oven to 180°C (350°F/Gas 4). Line 24 flat-bottomed patty holes with paper cases.

Cream the butter, sugar and vanilla with electric beaters until light and creamy. Add the eggs one at a time, beating well after each addition. Sift the flours together and fold in alternately with the plum juice. Divide the mixture evenly among the cases and cover each with slices of plum.

To make the crumble topping, place the sugar, flour and butter in a bowl. Mix together with your fingertips until it resembles coarse breadcrumbs. Sprinkle the crumble over each cake, covering the plums.

Bake for 15–18 minutes, or until golden. Transfer onto a wire rack to cool.

MAKES 24

185 g (6½ oz) unsalted butter, softened
170 g (6 oz/¾ cup) caster (superfine) sugar
1 teaspoon natural vanilla extract
3 eggs
125 g (4½ oz/1 cup) self-raising flour
30 g (1 oz/¼ cup) plain (all-purpose) flour
125 ml (4 fl oz/½ cup) tinned natural plum juice
9 tinned plums in natural juice, stones removed, thinly sliced

Crumble topping
110 g (3¾ oz/½ cup) raw (demerara) sugar
125 g (4½ oz/1 cup) plain (all-purpose) flour
100 g (3½ oz) unsalted butter, chilled and diced

9

Gingerbread cupcakes

MAKES 16

250 g (9 oz/2 cups) self-raising flour
90 g (3¼ oz/¾ cup) plain (all-purpose) flour
½ teaspoon bicarbonate of soda (baking soda)
3 teaspoons ground ginger
1 teaspoon ground cinnamon
1 teaspoon mixed spice
230 g (8½ oz/1 cup) soft brown sugar
55 g (2 oz/¼ cup) glacé ginger, chopped
235 g (8½ oz/⅔ cup) golden syrup or maple syrup
100 g (3½ oz) unsalted butter, chopped
250 ml (9 fl oz/1 cup) buttermilk
2 eggs, lightly beaten

Ginger icing (frosting)
250 g (9 oz/2 cups) icing (confectioners') sugar, sifted
1 teaspoon ground ginger
20 g (¾ oz) unsalted butter, softened

Preheat the oven to 200°C (400°F/Gas 6). Line 16 standard muffin holes with paper cases.

Sift the flours, bicarbonate of soda, ground ginger, cinnamon and mixed spice into a large bowl. Stir in the brown sugar and glacé ginger. Make a well in the centre.

Put the golden syrup and butter in a small saucepan and stir over medium heat until melted. Remove from the heat and cool. Combine the syrup mixture, the buttermilk and egg in a jug, mix together and pour into the well in the dry ingredients. Fold in gently until just combined — the batter should be lumpy.

Divide the mixture evenly among the cases. Bake for 20–25 minutes, or until a skewer comes out clean when inserted into the centre of a cake. Transfer onto a wire rack to cool.

To make the ginger icing, place the icing sugar, ginger and butter in a small heatproof bowl. Stir in enough warm water to form a smooth paste. Sit the bowl over a saucepan of simmering water, making sure the bowl doesn't touch the water, and stir until smooth and glossy. Remove from the heat. Spread 2 teaspoons of icing over each cake. Sprinkle with icing sugar.

Hot cross bun cakes

MAKES 12

250 g (9 oz/2 cups) self-raising flour
3 teaspoons ground cinnamon
125 g (4½ oz) unsalted butter, chopped
125 g (4½ oz/1 cup) sultanas (golden raisins)
45 g (1⅔ oz/¼ cup) mixed peel (mixed candied citrus peel)
170 g (6 oz/¾ cup) caster (superfine) sugar
185 ml (6 fl oz/¾ cup) milk
2 eggs, lightly beaten

Glaze
2 teaspoons powdered gelatine
2 tablespoons caster (superfine) sugar

Icing (frosting)
60 g (2¼ oz/½ cup) icing (confectioners') sugar
2 teaspoons lemon juice

Preheat the oven to 200°C (400°F/Gas 6). Grease 12 standard muffin holes.

Sift the flour and cinnamon into a large bowl, add the butter, then rub together with your fingertips until the mixture resembles fine breadcrumbs. Stir in the sultanas, mixed peel and caster sugar. Make a well in the centre.

Whisk the milk and egg in a jug, then pour into the well. Fold in gently until just combined — the batter should be lumpy.

Divide the mixture evenly among the muffin holes. Bake for 20–25 minutes, or until the cakes come away from the side of the tin. Cool briefly, then transfer onto a wire rack.

To make the glaze, combine the gelatine, caster sugar and 2 tablespoons of water in a small saucepan. Stir over low heat for 1 minute, or until the sugar and gelatine are dissolved. Remove from the heat. Brush the glaze over the warm cakes a couple of times, then allow them to cool.

To make the icing, mix the icing sugar and lemon juice together until smooth. Spoon the icing into a piping bag, and pipe a cross on each cake and allow them to set.

Jaffa cupcakes

MAKES 12

165 g (5¾ oz/1⅓ cups) self-raising flour
30 g (1 oz/¼ cup) unsweetened cocoa powder
220 g (7¾ oz/1 cup) caster (superfine) sugar
2 eggs, lightly beaten
170 ml (5½ fl oz/⅔ cup) milk
125 g (4½ oz/½ cup) unsalted butter, melted
1 tablespoon finely grated orange zest

Orange buttercream
250 g (9 oz/2 cups) icing (confectioners')
sugar, sifted
60 g (2¼ oz) unsalted butter, softened
2 teaspoons finely grated orange zest
2 tablespoons orange juice
orange cachous, to decorate

Preheat the oven to 180°C (350°F/Gas 4).
Line 12 standard muffin holes with paper cases.

Sift the flour and cocoa into a large bowl, then stir in
the sugar. Add the egg, milk, melted butter and
orange zest and beat with electric beaters for
2 minutes, or until well combined and smooth.

Divide the mixture evenly among the cases. Bake for
18–20 minutes, or until a skewer comes out clean when
inserted into the centre of a cake. Transfer onto a wire
rack to cool.

To make the orange buttercream, place 125 g (4½ oz/
1 cup) of the icing sugar, the butter, zest and orange
juice in a large mixing bowl. Beat with electric
beaters until smooth and creamy. Gradually add
the remaining icing sugar and beat until the cream
is thick.

Decorate each cake with buttercream and
orange cachous.

Apricot, sour cream and coconut cupcakes

Preheat the oven to 180°C (350°F/Gas 4).
Line 20 standard muffin holes with paper cases.

Sift the flour into a large mixing bowl, then add the coconut and make a well in the centre. Melt the butter and sugar in a small saucepan over low heat, stirring until the sugar has dissolved. Remove from the heat. Whisk the combined egg and apricot nectar into the sour cream. Add both the butter and the egg mixtures to the well in the dry ingredients and stir with a wooden spoon until combined.

Divide the mixture evenly among the cases and place an apricot half, cut side up, on the top of each cake. Bake for 18–20 minutes, or until a skewer comes out clean when inserted into the centre of a cake. Transfer onto a wire rack to cool.

Heat the jam in a small saucepan until melted. Brush a little jam over each cake.

MAKES 20

220 g (7¾ oz/1¾ cups) self-raising flour
45 g (1⅔ oz/½ cup) desiccated coconut
125 g (4½ oz) unsalted butter
230 g (8½ oz/1 cup) caster (superfine) sugar
2 eggs, lightly beaten
250 ml (9 fl oz/1 cup) apricot nectar
125 g (4½ oz/½ cup) sour cream
825 g (1 lb 13 oz) tinned apricot halves in juice, drained (you need 20 apricot halves)
80 g (2¾ oz/¼ cup) apricot jam

17

Butterfly cupcakes

120 g (4¼ oz) unsalted butter, softened
145 g (5 oz/⅔ cup) caster (superfine) sugar
185 g (6½ oz/1½ cups) self-raising flour
125 ml (4 fl oz/½ cup) milk
2 eggs
125 ml (4 fl oz/½ cup) thick
(double/heavy) cream
80 g (1½ oz/¼ cup) strawberry jam
icing (confectioners') sugar, to sprinkle

Preheat the oven to 180°C (350°F/Gas 4).
Line 12 standard muffin holes with paper cases.

Beat the butter, sugar, flour, milk and eggs with
electric beaters on low speed until combined. Increase
to medium speed and beat until the mixture is smooth
and pale.

Divide the mixture evenly among the cases and bake
for 15–20 minutes, or until a skewer comes out clean
when inserted into the centre of a cake. Transfer onto
a wire rack to cool.

Cut a shallow round from the centre of each cake using
the point of a sharp knife, then cut the round in half.
Spoon 2 teaspoons of cream into the cavity of each cake,
then top with 1 teaspoon of jam. Position the two
halves of the cake round in the jam to resemble
butterfly wings. Sprinkle with sifted icing sugar.

Peanut butter
mini cupcakes

MAKES 18

Preheat the oven to 180°C (350°F/Gas 4). Line 18 flat-bottomed patty holes with paper cases.

Beat the butter and sugar together in a bowl with electric beaters until light and creamy. Add the eggs, one at a time, beating well after each addition. Add the peanut butter and beat until combined. Fold in the sifted flours alternately with the milk until combined.

Divide the mixture evenly among the cases. Bake for 10–12 minutes, or until a skewer comes out clean when inserted into the centre of a cake. Transfer onto a wire rack to cool completely.

To make the hazelnut and peanut butter icing, combine the hazelnut spread and peanut butter. Spread the icing over each cake and decorate with a piece of chocolate peanut bar.

150 g (5½ oz) unsalted butter, chopped
115 g (4 oz/½ cup) soft brown sugar
2 eggs
125 g (4½ oz/½ cup) crunchy peanut butter
125 g (4½ oz/1 cup) self-raising flour
30 g (1 oz/¼ cup) plain (all-purpose) flour
60 ml (2 fl oz/¼ cup) milk

Hazelnut and peanut butter icing (frosting)
120 g (4¼ oz/½ cup) hazelnut spread, softened
90 g (3¼ oz/⅓ cup) crunchy peanut butter, softened
2 x 60 g (2¼ oz) chocolate-coated peanut bars (such as Snickers), chopped

Jam doughnut cupcakes

MAKES 18

155 g (5½ oz/1¼ cups) self-raising flour
115 g (4 oz/½ cup) caster (superfine) sugar
125 ml (4 fl oz/½ cup) milk
2 eggs
1 teaspoon natural vanilla extract
½ teaspoon dried yeast
160 g (5⅔ oz/½ cup) strawberry jam
20 g (¾ oz) unsalted butter, melted
2 tablespoons cinnamon sugar

Preheat the oven to 180°C (350°F/Gas 4).
Line 18 standard muffin holes with paper cases.

Combine the flour and sugar in a bowl, and make a well in the centre. Put the milk, eggs, vanilla and yeast in a jug and whisk to combine. Pour into the well in dry ingredients and whisk until smooth.

Divide half the mixture evenly among the cases. Top each with 1 teaspoon of jam, then cover with the remaining mixture. Bake for 10–12 minutes, or until a skewer comes out clean when inserted into the centre of a cake. Brush a little melted butter over each cake, then dip it into the cinnamon sugar. Serve the cakes warm.

Honey, banana and macadamia cupcakes

MAKES 32

Preheat the oven to 180°C (350°F/Gas 4). Line 32 mini muffin holes with paper cases.

Melt the butter and honey in a small saucepan, stirring until combined. Allow to cool.

Sift the flour and mixed spice into a large bowl. Add the carrot, banana, macadamias, eggs and honey mixture, stirring until the mixture is just combined and smooth.

Divide the mixture evenly among the cases, and sprinkle the tops liberally with extra chopped macadamias. Bake for 8 minutes, or until a skewer comes out clean when inserted into the centre of a cake. Transfer onto a wire rack to cool.

Drizzle a little honey over the cakes before serving.

100 g (3½ oz) unsalted butter, chopped
350 g (12 oz/1 cup) honey, plus extra to drizzle
250 g (9 oz/2 cups) self-raising flour
1 teaspoon mixed spice
150 g (5½ oz/1½ cups) coarsely grated carrot
1 ripe banana, mashed
70 g (2½ oz/½ cup) chopped macadamia nuts, plus extra, to sprinkle
2 eggs, lightly beaten

Neenish cupcakes

MAKES 16

250 g (9 oz) unsalted butter
230 g (8½ oz/1 cup) caster (superfine) sugar
1 teaspoon natural vanilla extract
4 eggs
185 g (6½ oz/1½ cups) self-raising flour, sifted
60 g (2¼ oz/½ cup) plain (all-purpose) flour, sifted
185 ml (6 fl oz/¾ cup) milk
30 g (1 oz/¼ cup) unsweetened cocoa powder, sifted

Icing (frosting)
185 g (6½ oz/1½ cups) icing (confectioners') sugar, sifted
10 g (¼ oz) unsalted butter

Chocolate topping
200 g (7 oz) dark chocolate, roughly chopped

Preheat the oven to 180°C (350°F/Gas 4).
Line 16 standard muffin holes with paper cases.

Beat the butter, sugar and vanilla together with electric beaters until light and creamy. Add the eggs, one at a time, beating well after each addition. Fold in the flours alternately with the milk. Divide the mixture in half and stir the cocoa through one half of the mixture until well combined. Divide the chocolate mixture evenly into half of the cases. Then divide the plain mixture into the other half, so that each case is filled with half chocolate and half plain mixtures. Bake for 18–20 minutes, or until a skewer comes out clean when inserted into the centre of a cake. Transfer onto a wire rack to cool.

To make the white icing, place the icing sugar and butter in a small heatproof bowl. Stir in enough warm water to form a smooth paste. Sit the bowl over a small saucepan of simmering water and stir until smooth and glossy. Remove from the heat. Spread the icing over the white side of each cake.

To make the chocolate topping, place the chocolate in a small bowl over a saucepan of simmering water, and stir occasionally until the chocolate has melted. Spread the chocolate over the other half of the cakes.

Apple pecan cupcakes

MAKES 16

Preheat the oven to 180°C (350°F/Gas 4). Line 16 standard muffin holes with paper cases.

Combine the flour, cinnamon, sugar, apple and pecans in a bowl. Add the egg, milk and melted butter, stirring until the mixture is just combined and smooth.

Divide the mixture evenly among the cases. Bake for 18–20 minutes, or until a skewer comes out clean when inserted into the centre of a cake. Transfer onto a wire rack to cool.

If desired, sprinkle with icing sugar and serve with thick cream or yoghurt.

310 g (11 oz/2½ cups) self-raising flour
1½ teaspoons ground cinnamon
165 g (5¾ oz/¾ cup) caster (superfine) sugar
2 granny smith's apples (about 340 g/11¾ oz), peeled, cored and coarsely grated
50 g (1¾ oz/½ cup) pecans, chopped
2 eggs, lightly beaten
125 ml (4 fl oz/½ cup) milk
15 g (½ oz) unsalted butter, melted
thick (double/heavy) cream or yoghurt, to serve (optional)

Beehive cupcakes

200 g (7 oz) unsalted butter, softened
185 g (6½ oz/1 cup) soft brown sugar
3 eggs
115 g (4 oz/⅓ cup) honey, warmed
280 g (10 oz/2¼ cups) self-raising flour, sifted

Marshmallow icing (frosting)
3 egg whites
330 g (11¾ oz/1½ cups) sugar
2 teaspoons light corn syrup
pinch of cream of tartar
1 teaspoon natural vanilla extract
yellow food colouring
15 toothpicks
15 chocolate-foil wrapped bumble bees
with wings

Preheat the oven 180°C (350°F/Gas 4). Line 15 standard muffin holes with paper cases.

Beat the butter and sugar with electric beaters until light and creamy. Add the eggs, one at a time, beating well after each addition. Fold in the honey and flour until combined. Divide the mixture evenly among the cases. Bake for 18–20 minutes, or until a skewer comes out clean when inserted into the centre of a cake. Transfer onto a wire rack to cool.

To make the marshmallow icing, combine the egg whites, sugar, corn syrup, cream of tartar and 100 ml (3½ fl oz) of water in a heatproof bowl. Sit the bowl over a saucepan of simmering water, making sure the bowl doesn't touch the water. Beat for 5 minutes with electric beaters, or until the mixture is light and fluffy. Remove from the heat. Add the vanilla and beat with electric beaters for 4–5 minutes, or until stiff peaks form. Add the colouring, drop by drop, and beat until just combined.

Spoon the icing into a piping bag fitted with a 1 cm (½ inch) round nozzle, and pipe the icing in circles around the cake to resemble a beehive. Push the pointy end of the toothpick into the base of each bee and insert it into each cake.

Mini pear and walnut cupcakes

MAKES 36

150 g (5½ oz) unsalted butter, softened
140 g (5 oz/¾ cup) soft brown sugar
2 eggs
155 g (5½ oz/1¼ cups) self-raising flour, sifted
125 ml (4 fl oz/½ cup) milk
135 g (3½ oz/½ cup) tinned pears, well drained
and chopped
40 g (1½ oz/⅓ cup) chopped walnuts

Maple cream icing (frosting)
90 g (3¼ oz) cream cheese, softened
60 ml (2 fl oz/¼ cup) maple syrup
185 g (6½ oz/1½ cups) icing (confectioners')
sugar, sifted
60 g (2¼ oz/½ cup) chopped walnuts,
to decorate

Preheat the oven to 180°C (350°F/Gas 4). Line 36 mini muffin holes with paper cases.

Beat the butter and sugar together with electric beaters until light and creamy. Add the eggs, one at a time, beating well after each addition. Fold in the flour alternately with the milk. Fold in the pears and the walnuts. Divide the mixture evenly among the cases. Bake for 12–15 minutes, or until a skewer comes out clean when inserted into the centre of a cake. Transfer onto a wire rack to cool.

To make the maple cream icing, beat the cream cheese and maple syrup with electric beaters until combined. Gradually beat in the icing sugar until combined. Spread the icing over each cake and decorate with chopped walnuts.

Milk chocolate buttons

MAKES 12

75 g (2½ oz) unsalted butter
75 g (2½ oz) milk chocolate, chopped
80 g (2¾ oz/⅓ cup) soft brown sugar
2 eggs, lightly beaten
60 g (2¼ oz/½ cup) self-raising flour, sifted

Ganache
80 g (2¾ oz) milk chocolate, chopped
2 tablespoons thick (double/heavy) cream
silver cachous, to decorate

Preheat the oven to 160°C (315°F/Gas 2–3). Line 12 mini muffin holes with paper cases.

Place the butter and chocolate in a heatproof bowl and sit the bowl over a saucepan of simmering water, making sure the bowl doesn't touch the water. Stir the chocolate until melted. Remove the bowl from the heat and mix in the sugar and egg. Stir in the flour.

Transfer the mixture to a jug and pour evenly among the cases. Bake for 20–25 minutes, or until cooked. Leave in the tin for 10 minutes, then transfer onto a wire rack to cool completely.

To make the ganache, place the chocolate and cream in a heatproof bowl. Sit the bowl over a saucepan of simmering water, making sure the bowl doesn't touch the water. Once the chocolate has almost melted, remove the bowl from the heat and stir until the remaining chocolate has melted and the mixture is smooth. Allow to cool for about 8 minutes, or until thickened slightly.

Return the cakes to the cold tin to keep them stable while you spread 1 heaped teaspoon of ganache over each cake. Decorate with silver cachous.

Banana sour cream cupcakes

MAKES 24

185 g (6½ oz) unsalted butter, softened
230 g (8½ oz/1 cup) caster (superfine) sugar
3 eggs
310 g (11 oz/2½ cups) self-raising flour
½ teaspoon bicarbonate of soda (baking soda)
185 g (6½ oz/¾ cup) sour cream
2 tablespoons maple syrup
3 very ripe bananas, mashed (about 300 g/10½ oz)

Honey cream icing (frosting)
80 g (2¾ oz) cream cheese, softened
50 g (1¾ oz) unsalted butter, softened
1½ tablespoons honey
250 g (9 oz/2 cups) icing (confectioners')
sugar, sifted

Preheat the oven to 180°C (350°F/Gas 4).
Line 24 standard muffin holes with paper cases.

Beat the butter and sugar in a large bowl using
electric beaters for 5–6 minutes, or until light and
fluffy. Add the eggs, one at a time, beating well after
each addition.

Sift the flour and bicarbonate of soda together. Add
the sour cream and maple syrup to the mashed
banana and mix well. Fold the flour mixture
alternately with the banana mixture in the butter
mixture until well combined.

Divide the mixture evenly among the cases. Bake for
15 minutes, or until a skewer comes out clean when
inserted into the centre of a cake. Transfer onto a wire
rack to cool.

To make the honey cream icing, place the cream cheese
and butter in a small bowl and beat with electric
beaters until smooth. Add the honey and icing sugar
and beat until smooth and well combined. Decorate
each cake generously with the icing.

Marble patty cakes

MAKES 10

Preheat the oven to 180°C (350°F/Gas 4).
Line 10 standard muffin holes with paper cases.

Beat the butter, sugar and vanilla together with electric beaters until light and creamy. Add the eggs, one at a time, beating well after each addition. Sift the flours together and fold in alternately with the milk.

Divide the mixture into three equal portions. Add a few drops of pink food colouring to one portion and mix to combine. Add the cocoa to another portion and mix to combine. Divide the three colours evenly into each case and gently swirl the mixture with a skewer. Bake for 15 minutes, or until a skewer comes out clean when inserted into the centre of a cake. Transfer onto a wire rack to cool.

To make the marble icing, mix the icing sugar, butter and enough hot water to make a spreadable icing. Spread the icing over each cake. Dip a skewer in pink food colouring and swirl it through the icing to create a marbled effect.

185 g (6½ oz) unsalted butter, softened
170 g (6 oz/¾ cup) caster (superfine) sugar
1 teaspoon natural vanilla extract
3 eggs
125 g (4½ oz/1 cup) self-raising flour
30 g (1 oz/¼ cup) plain (all-purpose) flour
125 ml (4 fl oz/½ cup) milk
pink food colouring
2 tablespoons unsweetened cocoa
   powder, sifted

Marble icing (frosting)
280 g (10 oz/2¼ cups) icing (confectioners')
   sugar, sifted
100 g (3½ oz) unsalted butter, softened
pink food colouring

Pecan and orange cupcakes

MAKES 16 or 24 mini

125 g (4½ oz) unsalted butter, softened
170 g (6 oz/¾ cup) caster (superfine) sugar
2 eggs
100 g (3½ oz/¾ cup) ground pecans
3 teaspoons finely grated orange zest
185 g (6½ oz/1½ cups) self-raising flour, sifted
125 ml (4 fl oz/½ cup) milk

Cinnamon icing (frosting)
15 g (½ oz) unsalted butter, softened
¾ teaspoon ground cinnamon
185 g (6½ oz/1½ cups) icing (confectioners')
sugar, sifted

Preheat the oven to 180°C (350°F/Gas 4).
Line 16 standard (or 24 mini) muffin holes with
paper cases.

Beat the butter and sugar with electric beaters until
pale and creamy. Gradually add the eggs, one at a
time, beating well after each addition. Add the ground
pecans and orange zest, then use a metal spoon to
gently fold in the flour alternately with the milk.

Divide the mixture evenly among the cases. Bake for
50–60 minutes (40 minutes for minis), or until a skewer
comes out clean when inserted into the centre of a
cake. Leave in the tin for 10 minutes, then transfer onto
a wire rack to cool.

To make the cinnamon icing, combine the butter,
icing sugar and cinnamon in a small bowl with
1½ tablespoons of hot water. Sit the bowl over a
saucepan of simmering water, making sure the bowl
doesn't touch the water, and stir until smooth and
glossy. Remove from the heat. Decorate each cake
with icing.

White chocolate chip cupcakes

MAKES 12

125 g (4½ oz) unsalted butter, softened
170 g (6 oz/¾ cup) caster (superfine) sugar
2 eggs
1 teaspoon natural vanilla extract
250 g (9 oz/2 cups) self-raising flour, sifted
125 ml (4 fl oz/½ cup) buttermilk
200 g (7 oz/1¼ cups) white chocolate chips

Preheat the oven to 170°C (325°F/Gas 3). Line 12 standard muffin holes with paper cases.

Beat the butter and sugar in a large bowl with electric beaters until pale and creamy. Gradually add the eggs, one at a time, beating well after each addition. Add the vanilla extract and beat until combined. Fold in the flour alternately with the buttermilk, then fold in the chocolate chips.

Divide the mixture evenly among the cases until three-quarters full. Bake for 20 minutes, or until a skewer comes out clean when inserted into the centre of a cake. Leave the cakes in the tin for 5 minutes, then transfer onto a wire rack to cool.

Rhubarb yoghurt cupcakes

MAKES 24

150 g (5½ oz/1½ cups) finely sliced fresh
rhubarb, plus 24 extra pieces to garnish
310 g (11 oz/2½ cups) self-raising flour, sifted
230 g (8½ oz/1 cup) caster (superfine) sugar
1 teaspoon natural vanilla extract
2 eggs, lightly beaten
125 g (4½ oz/½ cup) plain yoghurt
1 tablespoon rosewater
125 g (4½ oz) unsalted butter, melted

Preheat the oven to 180°C (350°F/Gas 4).
Line 24 standard muffin holes with paper cases.

Combine the rhubarb, flour and sugar in a bowl. Add
the vanilla, egg, yoghurt, rosewater and the melted
butter, stirring with a wooden spoon until the mixture
is just combined.

Divide the mixture evenly among the cases, then top
with a piece of rhubarb. Bake for 15 minutes, or until
a skewer comes out clean when inserted into the
centre of a cake. Transfer onto a wire rack to cool.

Apple and raisin cupcakes

MAKES 12

185 g (6½ oz/1½ cups) self-raising flour
150 g (5½ oz) unsalted butter, chopped
140 g (5 oz/¾ cup) soft brown sugar
125 g (4½ oz/1 cup) raisins, plus extra
   to garnish
120 g (4¼ oz) apple purée
3 eggs, lightly beaten

Yoghurt topping
250 g (9 oz/1 cup) plain yoghurt
1 tablespoon soft brown sugar

Preheat the oven to 180°C (350°F/Gas 4).
Line 12 standard muffin holes with paper cases.

Sift the flour into a large bowl and make a well in the
centre. Melt the butter and sugar in a small saucepan
over a low heat, stirring until the sugar has dissolved.
Remove from the heat. Combine the raisins and apple
purée with the butter mixture. Pour into the well
in the flour, along with the egg. Stir with a
wooden spoon until combined.

Divide the mixture evenly among the cases. Bake for
15 minutes, or until a skewer comes out clean when
inserted into the centre of a cake. Transfer onto a wire
rack to cool completely.

To make the yoghurt topping, combine the
yoghurt and sugar. Spread 1 tablespoon of
topping over each cake.

Long afternoon teas

These elegant offerings call for an aromatic brew
to be sipped slowly from your finest China cup.

Pistachio and cardamom cupcakes

MAKES 24

140 g (5 oz/1 cup) unsalted pistachio kernels
½ teaspoon ground cardamom, plus extra
to sprinkle
150 g (5½ oz) unsalted butter, chopped
185 g (6½ oz/1½ cups) self-raising flour
170 g (6 oz/¾ cup) caster (superfine) sugar
3 eggs
125 g (½ oz/½ cup) plain yoghurt

Lime syrup
115 g (4 oz/½ cup) caster (superfine) sugar
rind of 1 lime, white pith removed

Honey yoghurt topping
250 g (9 oz/1 cup) plain yoghurt
1 tablespoon honey

Preheat the oven to 180°C (350°F/Gas 4).
Line 24 standard muffin holes with paper cases.

Place the pistachios and cardamom in a food processor
and pulse until just chopped. Add the butter, flour
and caster sugar and pulse for 20 seconds, or until
crumbly. Add the eggs and yoghurt and pulse until
just combined.

Divide the mixture evenly among the cases. Bake for
15 minutes, or until a skewer comes out clean when
inserted into the centre of a cake. Transfer onto a wire
rack to cool.

To make the lime syrup, place the caster sugar and
100 ml (3½ fl oz) of water in a small saucepan and
stir over low heat until the sugar has dissolved.
Bring to the boil, then add the rind and cook for
5 minutes. Strain. Brush the syrup over the cakes
while they're still warm, and then allow to cool.

To make the honey yoghurt topping, place the
yoghurt and honey in a small bowl and stir until well
combined. Decorate each cake with the honey yoghurt
and a sprinkle of ground cardamom.

54

Fruit tart cupcakes

MAKES 12

Preheat the oven to 180°C (350°F/Gas 4). Line 12 standard muffin holes with paper cases.

Beat the butter, sugar and vanilla together with electric beaters until light and creamy. Add the eggs, one at a time, beating well after each addition. Sift the flours together and fold in alternately with the milk.

Divide the mixture evenly among the cases. Bake for 15 minutes, or until a skewer comes out clean when inserted into the centre of a cake. Transfer onto a wire rack to cool.

Cut the centre out of each cake, leaving a 1 cm (½ inch) border. Fill each cavity with 2 teaspoons of custard. Cut the fruit and arrange over the custard. Heat the jam until runny. Lightly brush the jam over the top of each cake. Refrigerate until ready to serve.

185 g (6½ oz) unsalted butter, softened
170 g (6 oz/¾ cup) caster (superfine) sugar
1 teaspoon natural vanilla extract
3 eggs
125 g (4½ oz/1 cup) self-raising flour
30 g (1 oz/¼ cup) plain (all-purpose) flour
125 ml (4 fl oz/½ cup) milk
125 g (4½ oz/½ cup) thick custard
1 kiwi fruit, peeled
125 g (4½ oz) strawberries
1 freestone peach, peeled
red grapes (about 4 to 6)
160 g (5⅔ oz/½ cup) apricot jam

Chocolate and almond cupcakes

MAKES 36

100 g (3½ oz) dark chocolate, chopped
50 g (1¾ oz/½ cup) ground almonds
90 g (3¼ oz/¾ cup) self-raising flour
4 eggs, separated
115 g (4 oz/½ cup) caster (superfine) sugar
2 tablespoons warm milk
chocolate flakes, to decorate
unsweetened cocoa powder, to sprinkle

Chocolate ganache
100 g (3½ oz) dark chocolate, chopped
100 g (3½ oz) unsalted butter

Preheat the oven to 180°C (350°F/Gas 4). Line 36 mini muffin holes with paper cases.

Place the chocolate in a food processor and process until finely ground. Add the ground almonds and flour and process until just combined.

Beat the egg yolks and sugar with electric beaters for 2–3 minutes, or until thick and pale. Stir in the chocolate mixture, then the milk. Beat the egg whites in a clean bowl until soft peaks form. Gently fold the whites into the mixture with a metal spoon until just combined. Divide the mixture evenly among the cases. Bake for 10–12 minutes, or until a skewer comes out clean when inserted into the centre of a cake. Transfer onto a wire rack to cool.

To make the chocolate ganache, place the chocolate and butter in a small heatproof bowl over a saucepan of simmering water, making sure the bowl doesn't touch the water. Stir until smooth and combined. Refrigerate for 20 minutes, stirring occasionally until thickened.

Cut the centre out of the cakes. Fill each cavity with 1 teaspoon of chocolate ganache, then decorate with chocolate flakes and cocoa.

Mandarin and chamomile cupcakes

MAKES 20

Preheat the oven to 180°C (350°F/Gas 4). Line 20 mini muffin holes with paper cases.

Place the milk and chamomile tea flowers into a saucepan and bring just to the boil. Stand for 5 minutes to infuse. Strain.

Place the butter, sugar, eggs, mandarin zest and mandarin in a food processor and process until almost smooth. Add the milk mixture, semolina and flour and process until smooth. Pour the mixture evenly among the cases. Bake for 8–10 minutes, or until a skewer comes out clean when inserted into the centre of a cake. Transfer onto a wire rack to cool.

To make the mandarin glaze, place the icing sugar, zest and enough juice to make a paste in a heatproof bowl. Sit the bowl over a saucepan of simmering water, making sure the base of the bowl doesn't touch the water, and stir until runny. Remove from the heat but keep the bowl over the water. Spread the glaze over each cake and decorate with a chamomile flower.

185 ml (6 fl oz/¾ cup) milk
5 g (⅛ oz/¼ cup) chamomile tea flowers, plus extra to decorate
150 g (5½ oz) unsalted butter, chopped
230 g (8½ oz/1 cup) caster (superfine) sugar
3 eggs
2 teaspoons finely grated mandarin zest
300 g (10½ oz) mandarin, peeled, seeds removed
60 g (2¼ oz/½ cup) fine semolina
155 g (5⅔ oz/1¼ cups) self-raising flour

Mandarin glaze
155 g (5½ oz/1¼ cups) icing (confectioners') sugar, sifted
1 teaspoon finely grated mandarin zest
2–3 tablespoons strained, fresh mandarin juice
chamomile tea flowers, to garnish

Individual blueberry cheesecakes

MAKES 6

Cheese mixture
115 g (4 oz/½ cup) caster (superfine) sugar
85 g (3 oz/⅓ cup) cream cheese

Blueberry sauce
250 g (9 oz/1⅔ cups) blueberries
1 tablespoon crème de cassis

165 g (5¾ oz/1⅓ cups) plain (all-purpose) flour
1 tablespoon baking powder
20 g (¾ oz) unsalted butter, melted
1 teaspoon finely grated orange zest
1 egg
125 ml (4 fl oz/½ cup) milk
18 blueberries, extra, for filling
icing (confectioners') sugar, to sprinkle

Preheat the oven to 180°C (350°F/Gas 4). Lightly grease 6 standard muffin holes with butter or oil.

To make the cheese mixture, put half the sugar in a bowl with the cream cheese and mix together well.

To make the blueberry sauce, put the blueberries in a blender or food processor with the liqueur and remaining sugar, and blend until smooth. Strain the mixture through a fine sieve to remove any blueberry seeds. Set the cheese mixture and sauce aside.

Sift the flour and baking powder together in a large bowl and stir in the butter, orange zest and ½ teaspoon of salt. In a separate bowl, beat the egg and milk together, then add to the dry ingredients and mix well until combined.

Divide half the mixture evenly among the holes. Add three of the extra blueberries and 1 teaspoon of cheese mixture in each hole, then top with the remaining batter mixture. Bake for 15 minutes, or until cooked and golden. Transfer onto a wire rack to cool slightly. To serve, put each cheescake on a plate, drizzle with blueberry sauce and sprinkle with icing sugar.

Prune and ricotta cupcakes

MAKES 18

Preheat the oven to 180°C (350°F/Gas 4). Line 18 mini muffin holes with paper cases.

Combine the prunes and Marsala in a small saucepan. Bring to the boil, then reduce the heat and simmer for 30 seconds, or until the Marsala is absorbed. Allow to cool.

Beat the ricotta and sugar with electric beaters for 2 minutes, or until light and creamy. Gradually add the eggs, one at a time, beating well after each addition. Add the cream and beat for 2 minutes. Using a metal spoon, fold in the sifted cornflour and flour, the prune mixture and the chocolate.

Divide the mixture evenly among the cases. Bake for 15–18 minutes, or until firm and lightly golden. Transfer onto a wire rack to cool. Sprinkle with icing sugar just before serving.

75 g (2⅔ oz/⅓ cup) pitted prunes, chopped
1 tablespoon Marsala
250 g (9 oz) ricotta cheese
115 g (4 oz/½ cup) caster (superfine) sugar
2 eggs
60 ml (2 fl oz/¼ cup) whipping cream
30 g (1 oz/¼ cup) cornflour (cornstarch), sifted
2 tablespoons self-raising flour, sifted
30 g (1 oz/¼ cup) grated dark chocolate

Orange and lemon syrup cupcakes

MAKES 36

125 g (4½ oz) unsalted butter, chilled and chopped
230 g (8½ oz/1 cup) caster (superfine) sugar
2 teaspoons finely grated lemon zest
2 teaspoons finely grated orange zest
3 eggs
125 ml (4 fl oz/½ cup) milk
185 g (6½ oz/1½ cups) self-raising flour, sifted

Lemon syrup
230 g (8½ oz/1 cup) caster (superfine) sugar
zest of 1 lemon, thinly sliced
zest of 1 orange, thinly sliced

Preheat the oven to 180°C (350°F/Gas 4). Line 36 mini muffin holes with paper cases.

Place the butter, sugar and lemon and orange zests in a saucepan and stir over low heat until the sugar has dissolved. Transfer to a large bowl. Add the eggs, milk and flour and beat with electric beaters until just combined.

Divide the mixture evenly among the cases. Bake for 15 minutes, or until a skewer comes out clean when inserted into the centre of a cake. Transfer onto a wire rack to cool.

To make the lemon syrup, place 200 ml (7 fl oz) of water and the sugar in a saucepan over a low heat, stirring until the sugar has dissolved. Add the lemon and orange zests, bring to the boil and simmer for 10 minutes, stirring occasionally, or until lightly golden and syrupy.

Strain the syrup, reserving the zest. Decorate each cake with some strips of zest and pour over a little of the syrup.

Fluffy coconut cupcakes

MAKES 36

Preheat the oven to 180°C (350°F/Gas 4). Line 36 mini muffin holes with paper cases.

Combine the flour, coconut and sugar in a bowl and make a well in the centre. Pour in the combined buttermilk, eggs, coconut extract and butter into the well and mix until combined.

Divide the mixture evenly among the cases. Bake for 12 minutes, or until a skewer comes out clean when inserted into the centre of a cake. Transfer onto a wire rack to cool.

To make the coconut icing, combine the icing sugar and coconut in a bowl. Add the butter, coconut extract and enough hot water to make a spreadable icing. Decorate each cake with a thick covering of icing and sprinkle with toasted coconut.

250 g (9 oz/2 cups) self-raising flour, sifted
45 g (1⅔ oz/½ cup) desiccated coconut
230 g (8½ oz/1 cup) caster (superfine) sugar
250 ml (9 fl oz/1 cup) buttermilk
2 eggs, lightly beaten
1 teaspoon natural coconut extract
125 g (4½ oz) unsalted butter, melted

Coconut icing (frosting)
280 g (10 oz/2¼ cups) icing (confectioners') sugar
135 g (4¾ oz/1½ cups) desiccated coconut
75 g (2½ oz) unsalted butter, softened
½ teaspoon natural coconut extract
2 tablespoons hot water
desiccated coconut, lightly toasted, to sprinkle

71

Hazelnut cream sponge cakes

MAKES 16

4 eggs, separated
115 g (4 oz/½ cup) caster (superfine) sugar
60 g (2¼ oz/½ cup) self-raising flour
75 g (2⅔ oz/⅔ cup) ground hazelnuts
20 g (¾ oz) unsalted butter

Hazelnut icing (frosting)
170 g (6 oz/½ cup) chocolate hazelnut spread
130 g (4¾ oz) unsalted butter, softened
60 g (2¼ oz/½ cup) icing (confectioners')
sugar, sifted

Preheat the oven to 180°C (350°F/Gas 4). Grease a shallow 20 cm (8 inch) square cake tin and line the base with baking paper.

Beat the egg whites in a clean bowl with electric beaters until soft peaks form. Gradually add the sugar, beating until thick and glossy. Beat the egg yolks into the mixture, one at a time.

Sift the flour over the mixture, add the ground hazelnuts and fold in with a metal spoon. Melt the butter with 2 tablespoons of boiling water in a small bowl, then fold into the sponge mixture. Pour the mixture into the tin and bake for 25 minutes, or until a skewer comes out clean when inserted into the centre of the cake. Leave in the tin for 5 minutes before turning out onto a wire rack to cool. Cut the sponge in half horizontally through the centre.

To make the hazelnut icing, beat the chocolate hazelnut spread and butter with electric beaters until very creamy. Beat in the icing sugar, then gradually add 3 teaspoons of boiling water and beat until smooth. Spread the icing over the base of the sponge, then replace the top layer. Refrigerate until the filling is firm, then cut into squares and place in paper cases.

Streusel cupcakes

MAKES 24

Preheat the oven to 180°C (350°F/Gas 4). Line 24 standard muffin holes with paper cases.

To make the custard, place the egg yolks, sugar and custard powder in a bowl and whisk until pale. Heat the milk in a small saucepan until almost boiling. Remove from the heat, then gradually whisk into the egg mixture. Return the combined mixture to the cleaned saucepan and stir constantly over low heat until the mixture boils and thickens. Refrigerate until cold.

To make the topping, mix all the ingredients together in a bowl, until the mixture resembles coarse breadcrumbs.

Beat the butter, sugar and vanilla together with electric beaters until light and creamy. Add the eggs, one at a time, beating well after each addition. Sift the flours and mixed spice together and fold in alternately with the sultanas and milk. Swirl the custard through the mixture, but do not overmix. Divide the mixture evenly among the cases. Sprinkle the topping over the cakes. Bake for 14–15 minutes, or until a skewer comes out clean when inserted into the centre of a cake. Transfer onto a wire rack to cool.

Custard
3 egg yolks
2 tablespoons caster (superfine) sugar
2 tablespoons custard powder
250 ml (9 fl oz/1 cup) milk
1 teaspoon natural vanilla extract

Topping
60 g (2¼ oz/½ cup) plain (all-purpose) flour
75 g (2⅔ oz) finely chopped walnuts
95 g (3¼ oz/½ cup) soft brown sugar
80 g (2¾ oz) unsalted butter, melted
1 teaspoon ground cinnamon

185 g (6½ oz) unsalted butter, softened
170 g (6 oz/¾ cup) caster (superfine) sugar
1 teaspoon natural vanilla extract
3 eggs
125 g (4½ oz/1 cup) self-raising flour
30 g (1 oz/¼ cup) plain (all-purpose) flour
1 teaspoon mixed spice
60 g (2¼ oz/½ cup) sultanas (golden raisins)
125 ml (4 fl oz/½ cup) milk

Passionfruit cupcakes

MAKES 15

185 g (6½ oz) unsalted butter, softened
170 g (6 oz/¾ cup) caster (superfine) sugar
1 teaspoon natural vanilla extract
3 eggs
125 g (4½ oz) cream cheese, softened
1 tablespoon fresh passionfruit pulp
(1 passionfruit)
125 g (4½ oz/1 cup) self-raising flour
30 g (1 oz/¼ cup) plain (all-purpose) flour
60 ml (2 fl oz/¼ cup) milk

Passionfruit icing (frosting)
300 ml (10½ fl oz) whipping cream
1½ tablespoons icing (confectioners') sugar, sifted
2 passionfruit, pulp removed

Preheat the oven to 180°C (350°F/Gas 4). Line 15 standard muffin holes with paper cases.

Beat the butter, sugar and vanilla together with electric beaters until light and creamy. Add the eggs, one at a time, beating well after each addition. Add the cream cheese and passionfruit and beat until smooth. Sift the flours together and fold in alternately with the milk.

Divide the mixture evenly among the cases. Bake for 15 minutes, or until a skewer comes out clean when inserted into the centre of a cake. Transfer onto a wire rack to cool.

To make the passionfruit icing, beat the cream and icing sugar together until soft peaks form. Cut the centre out of each cake leaving a 1 cm (½ inch) border. Spoon the cream into a piping bag fitted with a 1 cm (½ inch, no 7) star nozzle. Decorate each cake with piped cream and top with the passionfruit.

Baklava cupcakes

MAKES 36

Preheat the oven to 180°C (350°F/Gas 4).
Line 36 mini muffin holes with paper cases.

Combine the filling ingredients in a bowl
and set aside.

Beat the butter and sugar in a bowl with electric
beaters until light and creamy. Add the eggs, one at a
time, beating well after each addition. Fold in the
sifted flours alternately with the milk, and stir until
smooth and combined.

Divide half the mixture evenly among the cases.
Sprinkle half the filling over the mixture, then spoon
the remaining mixture over the top. Sprinkle over the
remaining filling. Bake for 10–12 minutes, or until a
skewer comes out clean when inserted into the centre
of a cake. Brush warm honey over the cakes while
they are still hot.

Filling
50 g (1¾ oz) walnuts, chopped
50 g (1¾ oz) blanched almonds, chopped
110 g (3¾ oz/½ cup) raw (demerara) sugar
2 teaspoons ground cinnamon
50 g (1¾ oz) unsalted butter, melted

185 g (6½ oz) unsalted butter, softened
140 g (5 oz/¾ cup) soft brown sugar
3 eggs
125 g (4½ oz/1 cup) self-raising flour
30 g (1 oz/¼ cup) plain (all-purpose) flour
125 ml (4 fl oz/½ cup) buttermilk
90 g (3¼ oz/¼ cup) honey, warmed

Plum and almond cupcakes

MAKES 18

185 g (6½ oz/1½ cups) self-raising flour
1½ teaspoons ground cinnamon
100 g (3½ oz) unsalted butter, melted
230 g (8½ oz/1 cup) soft brown sugar
3 eggs, lightly beaten
50 g (1¾ oz/⅓ cup) blanched almonds, finely chopped
825 g (1 lb 13 oz) tinned stoned plums in natural juice, drained and chopped
dried rose petals, to decorate

White chocolate cream icing (frosting)
200 g (7 oz) white chocolate, chopped
125 ml (4 fl oz/½ cup) pouring cream
200 g (7 oz) cream cheese, softened
40 g (2¾ oz/⅓ cup) icing (confectioners') sugar, sifted
pink food colouring

Preheat the oven to 160°C (315°F/Gas 2–3). Line 18 standard muffin holes with paper cases.

Sift the flour and cinnamon together in a bowl. Add the butter, sugar, eggs, almonds and plums and mix with electric beaters until combined.

Divide the mixture evenly among the cases. Bake for 15 minutes, or until a skewer comes out clean when inserted into the centre of a cake. Transfer onto a wire rack to cool.

To make the white chocolate cream icing, combine the chocolate and cream in a small saucepan and stir over low heat until the chocolate has melted. Place the chocolate mixture, cream cheese and icing sugar in a bowl and beat with electric beaters until smooth. Add a few drops of red food colouring and blend evenly. Cover the bowl and refrigerate for 2 minutes, or until slightly firm. Beat the mixture again for a few seconds until smooth.

Spread the icing over each cake and decorate with the dried rose petals.

Mango cakes with lime syrup

Preheat the oven to 200°C (400°F/Gas 6). Grease 8 large muffin holes, then line with the mango slices.

Beat the butter and sugar in a bowl with electric beaters until light and creamy. Gradually add the eggs, one at a time, beating well after each addition. Fold in the flour, then add the almonds and coconut milk.

Divide the mixture evenly among the holes. Bake for 25 minutes, or until a skewer comes out clean when inserted into the centre of a cake.

To make the lime syrup, place the lime juice, sugar and 125 ml (4 fl oz/½ cup) of water in a small saucepan and stir over low heat until the sugar dissolves. Increase the heat and simmer for 10 minutes.

Pierce holes in each cake with a skewer. Drizzle the syrup over the top and leave for 5 minutes to soak up the liquid. Turn out onto plates and serve.

MAKES 8

850 g (1 lb 14 oz) tinned mango slices in syrup, drained
180 g (6½ oz) unsalted butter, softened
120 g (8 oz/1 cup) caster (superfine) sugar
4 eggs
220 g (7¾ oz/1 cup) self-raising flour
4 tablespoons ground almonds
4 tablespoons coconut milk

Lime syrup
4 tablespoons lime juice
115 g (4 oz/½ cup) caster (superfine) sugar

Madeira cupcakes

180 g (6½ oz) unsalted butter, softened
170 g (6 oz/¾ cup) caster (superfine) sugar
3 eggs
165 g (5¾ oz/1⅓ cups) plain (all-purpose) flour
2 teaspoons baking powder
1 teaspoon finely grated orange zest
1 tablespoon orange juice

Orange icing (frosting)
250 g (9 oz/2 cups) icing (confectioners')
sugar, sifted
125 g (4½ oz) unsalted butter, softened
1 tablespoon orange juice

Preheat the oven to 180°C (350°/Gas 4).
Line 12 standard muffin holes with paper cases.

Beat the butter and sugar in a bowl, with electric
beaters until pale and light. Add the eggs,
one at a time, beating well after each addition.
Sift the flour and baking powder together. Fold the
flour, orange zest and juice into the butter mixture
until combined.

Divide the mixture evenly among the cases. Bake for
12–15 minutes, or until a skewer comes out clean when
inserted into the centre of a cake. Transfer onto a wire
rack to cool completely.

To make the orance icing, place the icing sugar, butter
and juice in a large bowl and beat with electric beaters
until smooth and well combined. Decorate each cake
with icing and sprinkle with icing sugar.

Chestnut cupcakes

MAKES 36

Preheat the oven to 180°C (350°F/Gas 4). Line 36 mini muffin holes with paper cases.

Beat the butter, sugar and vanilla with electric beaters until light and creamy. Add the chestnut purée and beat for 1 minute, or until just combined. Add the eggs, one at a time, beating well after each addition. Fold in the milk, flour and baking powder, and stir with a wooden spoon until the ingredients are just combined.

Divide the mixture evenly among the cases. Bake for 15 minutes, or until a skewer comes out clean when inserted into the centre of a cake. Transfer onto a wire rack to cool completely.

To make the chocolate glaze, combine the chocolate and cream in a small saucepan. Stir over low heat until the chocolate has melted and the mixture is smooth. Remove from the heat and cool slightly.

Dip the top of each cake into the glaze to coat and decorate each with an icing flower.

125 g (4½ oz) unsalted butter, softened
230 g (8½ oz/1 cup) caster (superfine) sugar
1 teaspoon natural vanilla extract
150 g (5½ oz/½ cup) unsweetened chestnut
  purée
3 eggs
80 ml (2½ fl oz/⅓ cup) milk
155 g (5⅔ oz/1¼ cups) self-raising flour, sifted
1 teaspoon baking powder
36 flower icing decorations

Chocolate glaze
250 g (9 oz) dark chocolate, chopped
185 ml (6 fl oz/¾ cup) pouring cream

Saffron spice cupcakes

MAKES 24

185 ml (6 fl oz/¾ cup) orange juice
3 teaspoons finely grated orange zest
¼ teaspoon saffron threads
2 eggs
125 g (4½ oz/1 cup) icing (confectioners') sugar
1 teaspoon natural vanilla extract
185 g (6½ oz/1½ cups) self-raising flour
155 g (5⅔ oz/1½ cups) ground almonds
100 g (3½ oz) unsalted butter, melted

Saffron threads
½ teaspoon saffron threads
2 tablespoons orange juice

Mascarpone cream
250 g (9 oz) mascarpone cheese
60 g (2¼ oz/½ cup) icing (confectioners')
sugar, sifted
¼ teaspoon ground cardamom

Preheat the oven to 180°C (350°F/Gas 4).
Line 24 standard muffin holes with paper cases.

Combine the orange juice, zest and saffron in a small saucepan and bring to the boil. Reduce the heat and simmer for 1 minute. Leave to cool.

Beat the eggs, icing sugar and vanilla with electric beaters until light and creamy. Fold in the sifted flour, almonds, orange juice mixture and butter with a metal spoon until combined. Divide the mixture evenly among the cases. Bake for 18–20 minutes, or until a skewer comes out clean when inserted into the centre of a cake. Transfer onto a wire rack to cool.

To make the saffron threads, place the saffron and orange juice in a small saucepan and bring to a simmer for 1 minute. Strain and discard the orange juice. Set the saffron threads aside.

To make the mascarpone cream, place the mascarpone, sugar and cardamom in a small bowl and mix to combine (be careful not to overmix or it may curdle). Decorate each cake with piped cream and top with the saffron threads.

Coconut, ginger and lime cupcakes

MAKES 36

Preheat the oven to 180°C (350°F/Gas 4). Line 36 mini muffin holes with paper cases.

Beat the butter, sugar and lime zest with electric beaters until light and creamy. Add the eggs, one at a time, beating well after each addition. Add the ginger. Stir in the sifted flour and the coconut alternately with the milk.

Divide the mixture evenly among the cases. Bake for 15 minutes, or until a skewer comes out clean when inserted into the centre of a cake. Transfer onto a wire rack to cool.

To make the lime icing, combine all of the ingredients, adding enough lime juice to make a smooth, runny icing. Decorate each cake with icing.

150 g (5½ oz) unsalted butter, softened
170 g (6 oz/¾ cup) caster (superfine) sugar
2 teaspoons finely grated lime zest
2 eggs
55 g (2 oz/¼ cup) finely chopped glacé ginger
215 g (7⅔ oz/1¾ cups) self-raising flour
45 g (1⅔ oz/½ cup) desiccated coconut
185 ml (6 fl oz/¾ cup) milk

Lime icing (frosting)
125 g (4½ oz/1 cup) icing (confectioners') sugar, sifted
10 g (¼ oz) unsalted butter, softened
1 teaspoon finely grated lime zest
2 tablespoons lime juice

Hawaiian macadamia cupcakes

MAKES 18

185 g (6½ oz/1½ cups) self-raising flour
½ teaspoon ground cinnamon
170 g (6 oz/¾ cup) caster (superfine) sugar
45 g (1⅔ oz/½ cup) desiccated coconut
3 eggs, lightly beaten
220 g (7¾ oz) tinned crushed pineapple
in syrup, drained
185 ml (6 fl oz/¾ cup) vegetable oil
50 g (1¾ oz) macadamia nuts, chopped,
plus extra to decorate

Lemon cream
90 g (3¼ oz) cream cheese, softened
45 g (1½ oz) unsalted butter, softened
1½ tablespoons lemon juice
280 g (10 oz/2¼ cups) icing (confectioners')
sugar, sifted

Preheat the oven to 180°C (350°F/Gas 4).
Line 18 standard muffin holes with paper cases.

Sift the flour and cinnamon into a large bowl, then
add the sugar and coconut and stir to combine. Add
the egg, pineapple and oil and mix well. Stir in the
macadamia nuts.

Divide the mixture evenly among the cases. Bake for
18–20 minutes, or until a skewer comes out clean
when inserted into the centre of a cake. Transfer onto
a wire rack to cool.

To make the lemon cream, beat the cream cheese and
butter in a large bowl with electric beaters until
smooth. Add the lemon juice and icing sugar, and beat
until well combined.

Decorate each cake with lemon cream and a
sprinkling of macadamia nuts.

Sour cherry cupcakes

MAKES 18

125 g (4½ oz) unsalted butter, softened
170 g (6 oz/¾ cup) caster (superfine) sugar
2 eggs
185 g (6½ oz/1½ cups) self-raising flour
125 ml (4 fl oz/½ cup) milk
200 g (7 oz/1 cup) pitted morello cherries,
   well drained, halved

Preheat the oven to 180°C (350°F/Gas 4). Line 18 standard muffin holes with paper cases.

Beat the butter and sugar with electric beaters until pale but not creamy. Add the eggs, one at a time, beating well after each addition. Fold in the sifted flour alternately with the milk. Gently fold in the cherries.

Divide the mixture evenly among the cases. Bake for 18–20 minutes, or until a skewer comes out clean when inserted into the centre of a cake. Transfer onto a wire rack to cool. Sprinkle with icing sugar before serving. These cakes are best eaten on the day they're made.

Sweet basil and olive oil cupcakes

MAKES 18

3 eggs
230 g (8½ oz/1 cup) caster (superfine) sugar
3 teaspoons finely grated orange zest
3 teaspoons finely grated lemon zest
185 ml (6 fl oz/¾ cup) olive oil
310 g (11 oz/2½ cups) self-raising flour
80 ml (2½ fl oz/⅓ cup) milk
80 ml (2½ fl oz/⅓ cup) orange juice

Creamy basil icing (frosting)
375 g (13 oz/3 cups) icing (confectioners')
sugar, sifted
90 g (3¼ oz) unsalted butter, softened
60 ml (2 fl oz/¼ cup) milk
1 teaspoon natural vanilla extract
2 tablespoons finely chopped basil,
plus small basil leaves to decorate

Preheat the oven to 180°C (350°F/Gas 4).
Line 18 standard muffin holes with paper cases.

Whisk the eggs and sugar in a large bowl until well combined. Add the orange and lemon zests, then stir in the olive oil. Stir in the sifted flour alternately with the milk and orange juice. Stir the mixture gently for 30 seconds with a wooden spoon.

Divide the mixture evenly among the cases. Bake for 15 minutes, or until a skewer comes out clean when inserted into the centre of a cake. Transfer onto a wire rack to cool.

To make the creamy basil icing, place half the icing sugar, butter, milk, vanilla and chopped basil in a large mixing bowl and beat with electric beaters until smooth and creamy. Gradually add the remaining icing sugar until the icing is thick. Decorate each cake with the icing and a small basil leaf.

Iced vovo cupcakes

Preheat the oven to 180°C (350°F/Gas 4).
Line 12 standard muffin holes with paper cases.

Beat the butter, sugar and vanilla together with electric beaters until light and creamy. Add the eggs, one at a time, beating well after each addition. Sift the flours together and fold in alternately with the milk. Gently stir through the jam, being careful not to overmix it. You want it to swirl through.

Divide the mixture evenly among the cases. Bake for 15 minutes, or until a skewer comes out clean when inserted into the centre of a cake. Transfer onto a wire rack to cool.

To make the pink icing, place the icing sugar and butter in a bowl and add enough hot water to make a spreadable consistency. Add a just few drops of food colouring to make a pale pink icing. Spread the icing over the cakes. Place the sieved jam in a piping bag fitted with a 1 cm (½ inch) plain nozzle. Pipe the jam down the centre of each cake, then sprinkle with the coconut.

MAKES 12

185 g (6½ oz) unsalted butter, softened
170 g (6 oz/¾ cup) caster (superfine) sugar
1 teaspoon natural vanilla extract
2 eggs
125 g (4½ oz/1 cup) self-raising flour
30 g (1 oz/¼ cup) plain (all-purpose) flour
125 ml (4 fl oz/½ cup) milk
3 tablespoons strawberry jam

Pink icing (frosting)
125 g (4½ oz/1 cup) icing (confectioners')
   sugar, sifted
10 g (¼ oz) unsalted butter, softened
pink food colouring
100 g (3⅔ oz/⅓ cup) strawberry jam, sieved
30 g (1 oz/⅓ cup) desiccated coconut, to sprinkle

Middle Eastern orange curd cupcakes

MAKES 24

90 g (3¼ oz/¾ cup) self-raising flour
60 g (2¼ oz/½ cup) fine semolina
55 g (2 oz/½ cup) ground almonds
1 teaspoon ground cardamom
170 g (6 oz/¾ cup) caster (superfine) sugar
125 g (4½ oz) unsalted butter, melted
2 eggs, lightly beaten
80 ml (2½ fl oz/⅓ cup) milk

Orange curd
2 egg yolks
1 egg
55 g (2 oz/¼ cup) caster (superfine) sugar
2 teaspoons finely grated blood orange zest
60 ml (2 oz) blood orange juice
75 g (2⅔ oz) unsalted butter
pistachio kernels, to decorate

Preheat the oven to 180°C (350°F/Gas 4).
Line 24 mini muffin holes with paper cases.

Place the sifted flour and semolina into a bowl with the almonds, cardamom and sugar. Make a well in the centre. Whisk the butter, egg and milk in a jug to combine. Pour into the well and mix until combined.

Divide the mixture evenly among the cases. Bake for 10–12 minutes, or until a skewer comes out clean when inserted into the centre of a cake. Transfer onto a wire rack to cool.

To make the orange curd, whisk the yolks, egg, sugar and zest together in a saucepan until combined. Add the juice and butter and whisk over a low heat for 2–3 minutes, or until the curd thickens. Transfer to a bowl and refrigerate until cold. Spread the curd over each cake and decorate with pistachios.

Dressed to impress

When only the best will do, a decadent selection
for the cupcake sophisticate.

Semolina berry cupcakes

MAKES 24

125 g (4½ oz/1 cup) fine semolina
60 g (2¼ oz/½ cup) self-raising flour, sifted
1 teaspoon baking powder, sifted
170 g (6 oz/¾ cup) caster (superfine) sugar
180 g (6½ oz) unsalted butter, melted
1 teaspoon natural vanilla extract
250 g (9 oz/1 cup) plain yoghurt
150 g (5½ oz) fresh raspberries (or frozen, thaw before use)

Sugared raspberries
240 g (8½ oz) fresh raspberries
1 egg white, lightly beaten
75 g (2⅔ oz/⅓ cup) caster (superfine) sugar

Icing (frosting)
125 g (4½ oz) unsalted butter, softened
185 g (6½ oz/1½ cups) icing (confectioners') sugar, sifted
2 teaspoons milk

Preheat the oven to 180°C (350°F/Gas 4).
Line 24 standard muffin holes with paper cases.

Place the semolina, flour, baking powder and sugar in a bowl. Combine the melted butter, vanilla and yoghurt, then add to the dry ingredients. Stir the mixture until smooth and just combined. Stir through the raspberries.

Divide the mixture evenly among the cases. Bake for 15 minutes, or until a skewer comes out clean when inserted into the centre of a cake. Transfer onto a wire rack to cool.

To make the sugared raspberries, lightly brush each berry with egg white, then dip in the sugar to coat. Place the raspberries on a baking tray lined with non-stick baking paper and set aside for 1 hour to dry.

To make the white icing, beat the butter, sugar and milk in a medium bowl using electric beaters until smooth and combined. Decorate each cake with the icing and top a sugared raspberry.

Rich dark chocolate cupcakes

MAKES 18

150 g (5½ oz) unsalted butter, chopped
200 g (7 oz) dark chocolate chips
185 g (6½ oz/1½ cups) self-raising flour
30 g (1 oz/¼ cup) unsweetened cocoa powder
285 g (10 oz/1¼ cups) caster (superfine) sugar
2 eggs, lightly beaten
chocolate curls, to decorate

Chocolate topping
250 g (9 oz) dark chocolate, chopped
40 g (1½ oz) unsalted butter

Preheat the oven to 160°C (315°F/Gas 2–3). Line 18 standard muffin holes with paper cases.

Place the butter and chocolate chips in a small heatproof bowl. Sit the bowl over a saucepan of simmering water, making sure the bowl doesn't touch the water. Stir the chocolate constantly until it is melted.

Sift the flour and cocoa into a large bowl. Combine the melted butter and chocolate mixture, sugar and egg, then add 185 ml (6 fl oz/¾ cup) of water and mix well. Add to the dry ingredients and stir until well combined. Divide the mixture evenly among the cases. Bake for 20–25 minutes, or until a skewer comes out clean when inserted into the centre of a cake. Transfer onto a wire rack to cool.

To make the chocolate topping, place the chocolate and butter in a small heatproof bowl and sit it over a saucepan of simmering water, making sure the base of the bowl doesn't touch the water. Stir the chocolate constantly until it melts. Decorate each cake with the topping and chocolate curls.

Strawberry swirl cupcakes

185 g (6½ oz) unsalted butter, softened
170 g (6 oz/¾ cup) caster (superfine) sugar
3 eggs
125 g (4½ oz/1 cup) self-raising flour
30 g (1 oz/¼ cup) plain (all-purpose) flour
125 ml (4 fl oz/½ cup) milk
¼ teaspoon pink food colouring

Liqueur strawberries
2 teaspoons icing (confectioners') sugar, sifted
1 tablespoon strawberry liqueur
6 strawberries, hulled and halved
small scoops strawberry ice cream

Preheat the oven to 180°C (350°F/Gas 4).
Line 12 standard muffin holes with paper cases.

Beat the butter and sugar together with electric beaters until light and creamy. Add the eggs, one at a time, beating well after each addition. Sift the flours together and fold in alternately with the milk. Add the food colouring and lightly swirl through the mixture to create a marbled effect.

Divide the mixture evenly among the cases. Bake for 15 minutes, or until a skewer comes out clean when inserted into the centre of a cake. Transfer onto a wire rack to cool.

Combine the icing sugar and liqueur and stir to dissolve the sugar. Add the strawberries and stir to combine. Set aside to macerate for 5 minutes.

Cut out the centre of each cake leaving a 1 cm (½ inch) border. Top each cake with a scoop of ice cream and decorate with a strawberry liqueur.

Sticky date cupcakes

MAKES 6

Preheat the oven to 180°C (350°F/Gas 4). Grease 6 large muffin holes.

Place the dates and 250 ml (4 fl oz/1 cup) of water in a saucepan and bring to the boil. Remove from the heat and stir in the bicarbonate of soda. Add the butter and stir until melted.

Sift the flour into a large bowl, then add the sugar and stir. Make a well in the centre. Add the date mixture and egg and stir until just combined. Divide the mixture evenly among the holes. Bake for 20 minutes, or until a skewer comes out clean when inserted into the centre of a cake. Allow to cool, then transfer onto serving plates.

To make the sauce, place the golden syrup, cream, butter and sugar in a small saucepan and stir over low heat for 3–4 minutes, or until the sugar has dissolved. Bring to the boil, then reduce the heat and simmer, stirring occasionally, for 2 minutes. Pierce the cakes a few times with a skewer, then drizzle with the sauce. Serve with a scooop of ice cream.

270 g (9½ oz/1½ cups) pitted dates, chopped
1 teaspoon bicarbonate of soda (baking soda)
60 g (2¼ oz) unsalted butter, chopped
185 g (6½ oz/1½ cups) self-raising flour
125 g (4½ oz/⅔ cup) soft brown sugar
2 eggs, lightly beaten
ice cream, to serve

Sauce
2 tablespoons golden syrup or maple syrup
185 ml (6 fl oz/¾ cup) pouring cream
90 g (3¼ oz) unsalted butter, chopped
140 g (5 oz/¾ cup) soft brown sugar

113

Decadent double choc mousse cupcakes

MAKES 24

90 g (3¼ oz/¾ cup) plain (all-purpose) flour
30 g (1 oz/¼ cup) self-raising flour
125 g (4½ oz) unsalted butter, chopped
230 g (8½ oz/1 cup) caster (superfine) sugar
100 g (3½ oz) white chocolate, chopped
1 egg
1 teaspoon natural vanilla extract
125 ml (4 fl oz/½ cup) milk

Chocolate mousse
1 egg yolk
2 tablespoons caster (superfine) sugar
500 ml (17 fl oz/2 cups) whipping cream
375 g (13 oz) dark chocolate chips, melted

Preheat the oven to 160°C (315°F/Gas 2–3).
Line 24 standard muffin holes with paper cases.

Sift the flours together in a bowl and make a well.
Place the butter, sugar and chocolate in a saucepan and
stir over low heat until the sugar has dissolved.
Remove from the heat and cool slightly.

Whisk the egg, vanilla and milk to combine, then
pour into the well in the flour, together with the
chocolate mixture, and whisk to combine. Divide the
mixture evenly among the cases, until half-full. Bake
for 15 minutes, or until a skewer comes out clean
when inserted into the centre of a cake. Transfer onto
a wire rack to cool completely.

To make the chocolate mousse, place the egg yolk and
sugar in a small bowl and whisk over a small saucepan
of simmering water until thick and creamy.

Beat the cream in a bowl with electric beaters until
soft peaks form. Add the melted chocolate and the egg
mixture and continue to beat for 1–2 minutes, or until
thickened. Decorate the cakes with the mousse, then
place them on a tray and refrigerate for 1 hour, or
until set. Sprinkle with cocoa before serving.

Flourless orange and almond dessert cupcakes

Place the whole oranges in a saucepan, cover with water and place a small plate on top to keep the oranges submerged. Gradually bring to the boil, then reduce the heat and simmer for 40 minutes, or until very soft.

Preheat the oven to 180°C (350°F/Gas 4). Line 24 standard muffin holes with paper cases.

Cut the oranges into quarters and leave to cool. Remove any pips, then blend in a food processor until very smooth. Add the ground almonds, sugar, baking powder, vanilla and liqueur and pulse until just combined. Add the egg and process again until just combined.

Divide the mixture evenly among the cases. Bake for 15–18 minutes, or until firm. Leave to cool in the tin.

To make the orange sour cream, whisk the sour cream, icing sugar and orange zest together until thickened. Decorate each cake with the icing and flaked almonds.

MAKES 24

2 oranges
155 g (10 oz/1½ cups) ground almonds
230 g (8½ oz/1 cup) caster (superfine) sugar
1 teaspoon baking powder
1 teaspoon natural vanilla extract
1 teaspoon Cointreau or orange-flavoured liqueur
6 eggs, lightly beaten
30 g (1 oz/⅓ cup) flaked almonds, lightly toasted, to decorate

Orange cream
500 g (1 lb 2 oz/2 cups) sour cream
125 g (4½ oz/1 cup) icing (confectioners') sugar, sifted
2 teaspoons finely grated orange zest

Turkish delight cupcakes

MAKES 36

185 g (6½ oz) unsalted butter, softened
345 g (12 oz/1½ cups) caster (superfine) sugar
3 eggs
185 g (6½ oz/1½ cups) self-raising flour
60 g (2¼ oz/½ cup) plain (all-purpose) flour
125 g (4½ oz/1 cup) unsweetened cocoa powder
125 ml (4 fl oz/½ cup) milk
3 x 76 g (2⅔ oz) bars chocolate-coated Turkish delight, cut into 1 cm (½ inch) pieces

Rosewater icing (frosting)
250 g (9 oz/2 cups) icing (confectioners') sugar, sifted
1 tablespoon rosewater
2 drops pink food colouring
Turkish delight (not chocolate coated), to decorate

Preheat the oven to 180°C (350°F/Gas 4). Line 36 mini muffin holes with paper cases.

Beat the butter and sugar together with electric beaters until light and creamy. Add the eggs, one at a time, beating well after each addition. Sift the flours and cocoa together and fold in alternately with the milk. Stir through the Turkish delight. Divide the mixture evenly among the cases. Bake for 18–20 minutes, or until a skewer comes out clean when inserted into the centre of a cake. Transfer onto a wire rack to cool.

To make the rosewater icing, place the icing sugar in a large bowl. Add the rosewater and 1½ tablespoons of boiling water, and stir until smooth (add a little more water if necessary to make a pouring consistency). Add the food colouring (add more food colouring if desired) and stir until well combined. Spread the icing over each cake, then decorate with pieces of Turkish delight.

Champagne jelly cupcakes

MAKES 36

150 g (5½ oz) unsalted butter, chopped
115 g (4 oz/½ cup) caster (superfine) sugar
1 teaspoon natural vanilla extract
2 eggs
185 g (6½ oz/1½ cups self raising flour, sifted
35 g (1¼ oz/⅓ cup) ground almonds
125 ml (4 fl oz/½ cup) milk
130 g (4½ oz/1 cup) fresh or frozen blackberries

Champagne jelly
750 ml (26 fl oz) bottle sparkling wine
2 tablespoons powdered gelatine
165 g (5¾ oz/¾ cup) sugar
36 fresh blackberries

Preheat the oven to 180°C (350°F/ Gas 4). Line 36 standard muffin holes with paper cases.

Beat the butter, sugar and vanilla with electric beaters until light and creamy. Add the eggs, one at a time, beating well after each addition. Fold in the flour and almonds alternately with the milk and blackberries until combined. Divide the mixture evenly among the cases until half-full. Bake for 10–12 minutes, or until a skewer comes out clean when inserted into the centre of a cake. Leave in the tins to cool.

To make the champagne jelly, place 500 ml (17 fl oz/ 2 cups) of the sparkling wine in a bowl and allow the bubbles to subside. Sprinkle over the gelatine. Place the remaining sparkling wine in a saucepan with the sugar and stir over low heat until the sugar dissolves. Remove from the heat, add the gelatine mixture and stir until the gelatine has dissolved. Refrigerate for 45 minutes, or until the jelly starts to set.

Decorate each cake with jelly and top with a blackberry. Refrigerate the cakes in the tins until set.

Lemon meringue cupcakes

MAKES 12

215 g (7⅔ oz/1¾ cups) self-raising flour
170 g (6 oz/¾ cup) caster (superfine) sugar,
plus extra to sprinkle
1 egg
1 egg yolk
170 ml (5½ fl oz/⅔ cup) milk
½ teaspoon natural vanilla extract
90 g (3¼ oz) unsalted butter, melted and cooled
200 g (7 oz/⅔ cup) ready-made lemon curd
2 egg whites

Preheat the oven to 200°C (400°F/Gas 6). Lightly grease 12 standard muffin holes.

Sift the flour into a large bowl and stir in 55 g (2 oz/ ¼ cup) of the caster sugar. Make a well in the centre.

Place the egg and egg yolk in a bowl and add a pinch of salt. Beat the eggs together, then stir in the milk, vanilla and butter. Pour the egg mixture into the well in the dry ingredients. Fold in gently until just combined — the mixture should be lumpy.

Divide the mixture evenly among the holes. Bake for 15 minutes — the cakes will only rise a little way up the holes. (Leave the oven on the same temperature.)

Cool the cakes in the tin for 10 minutes, then loosen with a knife but leave in the tin. Hollow out the centre of each cake with a melon baller, being careful not to pierce through the base of the cake.

Stir the lemon curd well, then spoon into a piping bag fitted with a 1 cm (½ inch) plain nozzle. Carefully pipe the curd into the cavity of each cake.

Whisk the egg whites in a clean dry bowl until soft peaks form. Add a quarter of the remaining sugar at a time, beating well after each addition, until stiff and glossy peaks form.

Place 1 heaped tablespoon of the meringue mixture on top of each cake and form peaks with the back of a spoon. Sprinkle a little of the extra caster sugar over the meringue.

Return the cakes to the oven for 5 minutes, or until the meringue is lightly golden and crisp and the cakes come away slightly from the side of the tin. Cool in the tin for 10 minutes, then carefully transfer onto a wire rack. The meringue topping might come off the cakes when they first come out of the oven, so handle the cakes carefully. The meringues will adhere to the cakes as they cool.

Serve warm or at room temperature. The cakes are best eaten on the day they are made so that the meringue stays crispy.

VARIATION: You can also use other flavours of citrus curds, such as lime or orange, to fill the cakes.

Pretty in pink butter cupcakes

MAKES 16

Preheat the oven to 180°C (350°F/Gas 4). Line 16 muffin holes with paper cases.

Beat the butter and sugar with electric beaters until light and creamy. Add the eggs, one at a time, beating well after each addition. Add the vanilla and beat until combined. Sift the flours together and fold in alternately with the milk. Stir until the ingredients are just combined and the mixture is almost smooth.

Divide the mixture evenly among the cases. Bake for 15–18 minutes, or until a skewer comes out clean when inserted into the centre of a cake. Transfer onto a wire rack to cool.

To make the buttercream, beat the butter and icing sugar with electric beaters until smooth and combined. Add the cream and beat for 30 seconds, or until fluffy. Add a few drops of pink food colouring and stir until well combined and the desired pink is achieved. Decorate each cake with the buttercream and silver cachous.

185 g (6½ oz) unsalted butter, softened
170 g (6 oz/¾ cup) caster (superfine) sugar
3 eggs
1 teaspoon natural vanilla extract
155 g (5⅔ oz/1¼ cups) self-rasing flour
30 g (1 oz/¼ cup) plain (all-purpose) flour
125 ml (4 fl oz/½ cup) milk
silver cachous, to decorate

Buttercream
250 g (9 oz) unsalted butter, softened
250 g (9 oz/2 cups) icing (confectioners') sugar, sifted
80 ml (2½ fl oz/⅓ cup) whipping cream
pink food colouring

Croquembouche cupcakes

MAKES 16

Puffs
155 g (5⅔ oz/1¼ cups) plain (all-purpose) flour
80 g (2¾ oz) unsalted butter
5 eggs

Filling
250 ml (9 fl oz/1 cup) milk
2 egg yolks
2 tablespoons caster (superfine) sugar
2 tablespoons plain (all-purpose) flour
1½ tablespoons Grand Marnier
185 ml (6 fl oz/¾ cup) whipping cream, whipped

Cupcakes
185 g (6½ oz) unsalted butter, softened
170 g (6 oz/¾ cup) caster (superfine) sugar
1 teaspoon natural vanilla extract
3 eggs
125 g (4½ oz/1 cup) self-raising flour
60 g (2¼ oz/½ cup) plain (all-purpose) flour
125 ml (4 fl oz/½ cup) milk

Toffee
350 g (12 oz/1½ cups) caster (superfine) sugar

Preheat the oven to 210°C (415°F/Gas 6–7). Line baking trays with baking paper.

To make the puffs, sift the flour three times onto a piece of baking paper. Place the butter in a saucepan with 310 ml (10¾ fl oz/1¼ cups) of water and stir until the mixture comes to the boil. Remove from the heat. Add the flour and beat until combined. Return to the heat and beat with a wooden spoon until the mixture forms a ball and leaves the side of the pan. Transfer to a large bowl and cool slightly. Add the eggs, one at a time, beating well after each addition until the mixture is thick and glossy.

Pipe heaped teaspoons of the mixture onto the baking trays, leaving room for spreading (you need 48 puffs). Sprinkle the mixture with a little water and bake for 10 minutes, or until browned. Make a small hole in the base of each puff. Reduce the heat to 180°C (350°F/Gas 4) and bake for a further 5 minutes to dry out.

130

To make the filling, place the milk in a saucepan and bring just to the boil. Remove from the heat and cool slightly. Beat the eggyolks, sugar and flour in a bowl until thick and pale. Gradually whisk in the milk. Return to a clean saucepan and stir over medium heat until the mixture boils and thickens. Remove from the heat and stir through the Grand Marnier. Cover the surface with plastic wrap and refrigerate until cold. Fold in the whipped cream.

To make the cupcakes, line 16 standard muffin holes with paper cases. Beat the butter, sugar and vanilla together with electric beaters until light and creamy. Add the eggs, one at a time, beating well after each addition. Sift the flours together and fold in alternately with the milk.

Divide the mixture evenly among the cases. Bake for 15 minutes, or until a skewer comes out clean when inserted into the centre of a cake. Transfer onto a wire rack to cool.

Cut the tops of the cakes to make them flat. Spoon the filling into a piping bag fitted with a 1 cm (½ inch) round nozzle. Pipe the filling into the holes in the puffs. Arrange the puffs in a pyramid shape on the top of each cake, using the filling to stick them together.

To make the toffee, place the sugar and 170 ml (5½ fl oz/ ⅔ cup) of water into a small saucepan and stir over low heat until the sugar has dissolved. Bring to the boil, then reduce the heat slightly and cook for 10 minutes without stirring, or until golden. Remove from the heat and drizzle the toffee the puffs.

White chocolate and macadamia cupcakes

MAKES 12

Preheat the oven to 180°C (350°F/Gas 4). Line 12 standard muffin holes with paper cases.

Beat the butter, sugar and vanilla together with electric beaters until light and creamy. Add the eggs, one at a time, beating well after each addition. Sift the flours together and fold in alternately with the milk, chocolate and macadamia.

Divide the mixture evenly among the cases. Bake for 15 minutes, or until a skewer comes out clean when inserted into the centre of a cake. Transfer onto a wire rack to cool.

To make the royal icing, beat the icing sugar and egg whites together for 5 minutes until white and glossy. Decorate each cake with the icing and little icing decorations.

185 g (6½ oz) unsalted butter, softened
170 g (6 oz/¾ cup) caster (superfine) sugar
1 teaspoon natural vanilla extract
3 eggs
125 g (4½ oz/1 cup) self-raising flour
30 g (1 oz/¼ cup) plain (all-purpose) flour
125 ml (4 fl oz/½ cup) milk
100 g (3½ oz) white chocolate, chopped
80 g (2¾ oz/½ cup) macadamia nuts, chopped
ready-made icing decorations, such as
   tiny butterflies

Royal icing (frosting)
250 g (9 oz/2 cups) icing (confectioners')
   sugar, sifted
2 egg whites

Chocolate cherry cupcakes

MAKES 12

4 x 55 g (2 oz) coated cherry bars, chopped
250 g (9 oz) unsalted butter, chopped
230 g (8½ oz/1 cup) soft brown sugar
1 teaspoon natural vanilla extract
155 g (5⅔ oz/1¼ cups) self-raising flour
2 tablespoons unsweetened cocoa powder
45 g (1⅔ oz/½ cup) desiccated coconut
3 eggs
12 fresh cherries, to decorate

Chocolate icing (frosting)
250 g (9 oz/2 cups) icing (confectioners')
sugar, sifted
60 g (2¼ oz/½ cup) unsweetened
cocoa powder
20 g (¾ oz) unsalted butter, softened

Preheat the oven to 160°C (315°F/Gas 2–3).
Line 12 standard muffin holes with paper cases.

Place the cherry bars, butter, sugar and vanilla in
a heatproof bowl. Sit the bowl over a saucepan of
simmering water, making sure the bowl doesn't touch
the water, and stir until the chocolate has melted.

Sift the flour and cocoa powder into a large bowl, then
add the coconut. Add the chocolate mixture and the
eggs and mix until combined.

Divide the mixture evenly among the cases. Bake for
18–20 minutes, or until a skewer comes out clean
when inserted into the centre of a cake. Transfer onto
a wire rack to cool.

To make the chocolate icing, place the icing sugar and
cocoa into a large bowl. Add the butter and enough
boiling water to make a smooth and spreadable
consistency. Spread the icing over each cake and
decorate with a cherry.

Rum and raisin cupcakes

MAKES 24

Preheat the oven to 180°C (350°F/Gas 4). Line 24 mini muffin holes with paper cases.

Combine the raisins, rum and extra 1 tablespoon of brown sugar in a small saucepan. Bring to the boil, then reduce the heat and simmer for 30 seconds, or until the rum has absorbed. Set aside to cool.

Beat the butter and brown sugar with electric beaters until pale and creamy. Add the egg — the mixture may look curdled but once you add the flour, it will bring it back together. Use a metal spoon to fold the sifted flour and buttermilk in two batches. Fold in the raisin and rum mixture.

Divide the mixture evenly among the cases. Bake for 15 minutes, or until a skewer comes out clean when inserted into the centre of a cake. Transfer onto a wire rack to cool.

To make the rum buttercream, dissolve the coffee in 1 tablespoon of boiling water. Beat the butter and icing sugar with electric beaters until light and creamy. Add half the rum and the coffee mixture and beat for 2 minutes, or until smooth and fluffy. Soak the raisins in the remaining rum. Decorate each cake with the icing and top with a raisin.

125 g (4½ oz/1 cup) raisins
60 ml (2 fl oz/¼ cup) rum
140 g (5 oz/¾ cup) soft brown sugar,
    1 tablespoon extra
185 g (6½ oz) unsalted butter, softened
2 eggs, lightly beaten
250 g (9 oz/2 cups) self-raising flour, sifted
125 ml (4 fl oz/½ cup) buttermilk
24 raisins, to decorate

Rum buttercream
2 teaspoons instant coffee granules
250 g (9 oz) unsalted butter, softened
375 g (13 oz/3 cups) icing (confectioners')
    sugar, sifted
60 ml (2 fl oz/¼ cup) rum

Chocolate cupcakes with ice cream

MAKES 10

185 g (6 oz) unsalted butter
330 g (11¾ oz) caster (superfine) sugar
2½ teaspoons natural vanilla extract
3 eggs
5 g (2½ oz/⅔ cup) self-raising flour, sifted
220 g (7¾ oz/1¾ cups) plain (all-purpose) flour, sifted
1½ teaspoons bicarbonate of soda (baking soda), sifted
90 g (3 oz/¾ cup) unsweetened cocoa powder
250 ml (9 fl oz/1 cup) buttermilk
small scoops vanilla ice cream

Preheat the oven to 180°C (350°F/Gas 4). Lightly grease 10 standard muffin holes with melted butter or oil.

Beat the butter and sugar with electric beaters until light and creamy. Beat in the vanilla. Add the eggs, one at a time, beating well after each addition.

Fold in the combined flours, bicarbonate of soda and cocoa powder with a metal spoon, alternately with the buttermilk. Stir until just smooth.

Divide the mixture evenly among the holes. Bake for 25 minutes, or until a skewer comes out clean when inserted into the centre of a cake. Leave the cakes to cool in the tins for 5 minutes, then transfer onto a wire rack to cool completely.

Cut out the centre of each cake, leaving a 1 cm (½ inch) border around the top. Keep the tops of the cakes to one side. Fill the centre of each cake with a small scoop of ice cream, then decorate with the cake top.

Frangipani cupcakes

MAKES 16

Preheat the oven to 180°C (350°F/Gas 4). Line 16 standard muffin holes with large cases.

Beat the butter, sugar and vanilla together with electric beaters until light and creamy. Add the eggs, one at a time, beating well after each addition. Sift the flours together and fold in alternately with the milk. Stir through the mallow bakes until combined.

Divide the mixture evenly among the cases. Bake for 15 minutes, or until a skewer comes out clean when inserted into the centre of a cake. Transfer onto a wire rack to cool.

To make the icing, beat the icing sugar and egg whites together for 5 minutes until white and fluffy. Divide the icing evenly into two separate bowls. Colour one with food colouring to make a pale pink.

Decorate half the cakes with pink icing and arrange white marshmallow quarters to resemble a flower on each cake. Repeat with the white icing and pink marshmallows for the remaining cakes. Squeeze a dollop of the yellow gel in the centre of all the marshmallow petals.

185 g (6½ oz) unsalted butter, softened
170 g (6 oz/¾ cup) caster (superfine) sugar
1 teaspoon vanilla extract
3 eggs
125 g (4½ oz/1 cup) self-raising flour
60 g (2¼ oz/½ cup) plain (all-purpose) flour
125 ml (4 fl oz/½ cup) milk
45 g (1½ oz/1 cup) pink and white mallow bakes
8 white marshmallows, quartered
8 pink marshmallows, quartered
yellow decorating gel

Icing (frosting)
375 g (13 oz/3 cups) icing (confectioners') sugar, sifted
2 egg whites
pink food colouring

143

Mint slice cakes

MAKES 12

185 g (6½ oz) unsalted butter, softened
170 g (6 oz/¾ cup) caster (superfine) sugar
1 teaspoon natural vanilla extract
3 eggs
125 g (4½ oz/1 cup) self-raising flour
30 g (1 oz/¼ cup) plain (all-purpose) flour
60 g (2¼ oz/½ cup) unsweetened cocoa powder
125 ml (4 fl oz/½ cup) milk

Peppermint cream
60 ml (2 fl oz/¼ cup) pouring cream
2 teaspoons vegetable oil
1 tablespoon liquid glucose
250 g (9 oz/2 cups) icing (confectioners')
sugar, sifted
peppermint extract

Ganache
125 g (4½ oz) dark chocolate, chopped
80 ml (2½ fl oz/⅓ cup) pouring cream

To make the peppermint cream, combine all of the ingredients except the peppermint extract in a saucepan. Stir over low heat until the mixture is smooth and creamy. Add a few drops of peppermint and mix well. Refrigerate until ready to use.

Preheat the oven to 180°C (350°F/Gas 4).
Line 12 standard muffin holes with paper cases.

Beat the butter, sugar and vanilla together with electric beaters until light and creamy. Add the eggs, one at a time, beating well after each addition. Sift the flours and cocoa together and fold in alternately with the milk. Divide the mixture evenly among the cases. Bake for 15 minutes, or until a skewer comes out clean when inserted into the centre of a cake. Transfer onto a wire rack to cool.

Remove the cakes from the cases and cut in half horizontally. Spread the bottom layers with peppermint cream, then replace the top layers.

To make the ganache, combine the chocolate and cream in a small saucepan. Stir over low heat until the chocolate has melted. Remove from the heat and cool. Decorate the cakes with the ganache. Keep the cakes refrigerated until ready to serve.

Caramel toffee cupcakes

Preheat the oven to 180°C (350°F/Gas 4). Line 12 standard muffin holes with paper cases.

Beat the butter and sugar together with electric beaters until light and creamy. Add the eggs, one at a time, beating well after each addition. Add the caramel and beat until combined. Sift the flours together and fold in alternately with the milk. Divide the mixture evenly among the cases. Bake for 15 minutes, or until a skewer comes out clean when inserted into the centre of a cake. Transfer onto a wire rack to cool.

To make the caramel icing, beat all of the ingredients with electric beaters until smooth. Refrigerate until ready to use.

To make the toffee, line a tray with non-stick baking paper. Place the sugar and lemon juice in a small heavy-based saucepan over low heat, shaking the pan occasionally, until the sugar melts and becomes a light caramel. Pour the toffee onto the tray and spread out very thinly. Set aside to cool and harden.

Spread the caramel icing over the cakes. Peel the paper away from the toffee and break into shards. Decorate each cake with some toffee shards.

MAKES 12

185 g (6½ oz) unsalted butter, softened
170 g (6 oz/¾ cup) caster (superfine) sugar
3 eggs
300 g (10½ oz/1 cup) ready-made thick, caramel filling
125 g (4½ oz/1 cup) self-raising flour
30 g (1 oz/¼ cup) plain (all-purpose) flour
2 tablespoons milk

Caramel icing (frosting)
185 g (6½ oz/1½ cups) icing (confectioners') sugar, sifted
20 g (¾ oz) unsalted butter, softened
150 g (5½ oz/½ cup) ready-made thick, caramel filling

Toffee
115 g (4 oz/½ cup) caster (superfine) sugar
1 tablespoon lemon juice

147

Mini Christmas pudding cakes

MAKES 12

500 g (1 lb 2 oz/4 cups) sultanas
(golden raisins)
375 g (13 oz/3 cups) raisins, chopped
250 g (9 oz/1⅔ cups) currants
240 g (8 oz/1 cup) quartered glacé cherries
250 ml (9 fl oz/1 cup) brandy or rum,
plus 1 tablespoon to glaze
250 g (9 oz) unsalted butter
230 g (7½ oz/1 cup) soft dark brown sugar
2 tablespoons apricot jam
2 tablespoons light treacle or golden syrup
1 tablespoon finely grated lemon
or orange zest
4 eggs
350 g (12 oz/2¾ cups) plain (all-purpose) flour
1 teaspoon each of ginger, mixed spice
and ground cinnamon
silver cachous, to decorate

Royal icing (frosting)
1 egg white
250 g (9 oz/2 cups) pure icing (confectioners')
sugar, sifted
2–3 teaspoons lemon juice

Put the fruit in a bowl with the brandy and leave to soak overnight.

Preheat the oven to 150°C (300°F/Gas 2). Lightly grease 12 mini muffin holes and line the bases with a circle of baking paper.

Beat the butter and sugar to just combine. Beat in the jam, treacle and zest. Add the eggs, one at a time, beating after each addition.

Stir the soaked fruit and the combined sifted flour and spices alternately into the butter mixture. Divide the mixure evenly among the holes, right to the top, smoothing the top. Bake for 40 minutes, or until a skewer comes out clean when inserted into the centre of a cake. Cool in the tins, then turn out cakes onto a wire rack so that the base becomes the top.

To make the royal icing, lightly beat the egg white with a wooden spoon. Gradually add the icing sugar, beating to a smooth paste. Slowly add enough of the lemon juice until slightly runny. Decorate each cake with the icing, using a palette knife to smooth, and letting some drizzle down the sides. Decorate with silver cachous.

Cream brûlée cupcakes

MAKES 12

185 g (6½ oz) unsalted butter, softened
170 g (6 oz/¾ cup) caster (superfine) sugar
1 teaspoon natural vanilla extract
3 eggs
125 g (4½ oz/1 cup) self-raising flour
30 g (1 oz/¼ cup) plain (all-purpose) flour
125 ml (4 fl oz/½ cup) milk
45 g (1⅔ oz/¼ cup) soft brown sugar

Cream filling
375 ml (13 fl oz/1½ cups) milk
3 egg yolks
55 g (2 oz/¼ cup) caster (superfine) sugar
2 tablespoons plain (all-purpose) flour

Preheat the oven to 180°C (350°F/Gas 4). Line 12 standard muffin holes with paper cases.

Beat the butter, sugar and vanilla together with electric beaters until light and creamy. Add the eggs, one at a time, beating well after each addition. Sift the flours together and fold in alternately with the milk. Divide the mixture evenly among the cases. Bake for 15 minutes, or until a skewer comes out clean when inserted into the centre of a cake. Transfer onto a wire rack to cool.

To make the cream filling, place the milk in a saucepan and bring just to the boil. Remove from the heat. Beat the egg yolks, sugar and flour until thick and pale. Gradually whisk in the milk. Return to the saucepan and stir over medium heat until the mixture boils and thickens. Remove from the heat.

Cut out the centre of the cakes, leaving a 1 cm (½ inch) border. Fill in the cavity of the cakes with the cream filling. Refrigerate until cold. Sprinkle 1 teaspoon of the brown sugar over each cake and place under a hot grill (broiler) for 3 minutes, or until caramelised.

Green tea cupcakes

125 ml (4 fl oz/½ cup) milk
3 teaspoons matcha (fine green tea powder)
185 g (6½ oz) unsalted butter, softened
170 g (6 oz/¾ cup) caster (superfine) sugar
1 teaspoon natural vanilla extract
3 eggs
125 g (4½ oz/1 cup) self-raising flour
30 g (1 oz/¼ cup) plain (all-purpose) flour
45 g (1⅔ oz/¼ cup) Japanese sweet red beans,
to decorate

Cream
250 ml (9 fl oz/1 cup) whipping cream
2 tablespoons icing (confectioners') sugar, sifted

Preheat the oven to 180°C (350°F/Gas 4).
Line 24 standard muffin holes with paper cases.

Place the milk in a saucepan and bring just to the boil.
Remove from the heat and whisk in the matcha.
Allow to cool.

Beat the butter, sugar and vanilla together with electric beaters until light and creamy. Add the eggs, one at a time, beating well after each addition. Sift the flours together and fold in alternately with the milk mixture. Divide the mixture evenly among the cases. Bake for 10–12 minutes, or until a skewer comes out clean when inserted into the centre of a cake. Transfer onto a wire rack to cool.

Beat the cream and icing sugar until stiff peaks form. Decorate each cake with cream and sweet red beans.

Truffle cupcakes

MAKES 18

Preheat the oven to 160°C (315°F/Gas 2–3). Line 18 standard muffin holes with paper cases.

Place the butter, chocolate and liqueur in a saucepan and stir over low heat until melted. Remove from the heat.

Sift the flours, cocoa and bicarbonate of soda into a large bowl. Stir in the sugar and make a well in the centre. Add the combined eggs, oil and milk and gradually pour into the well, along with the chocolate mixture, mixing until combined. Divide the mixture evenly among the cases until three-quarters full. Bake for 25 minutes, or until a skewer comes out clean when inserted into the centre of a cake. Transfer onto a wire rack to cool.

To make the milk chocolate ganache, place all of the ingredients in a saucepan and stir over low heat until melted. Transfer to a bowl and allow to cool completely. Beat with electric beaters until thick and creamy. Decorate each cake with the ganache and a piece of truffle. Sprinkle with cocoa to serve.

200 g (7 oz) unsalted butter
200 g (7 oz) dark chocolate, chopped
125 ml (4 fl oz/½ cup) coffee liqueur
90 g (3 oz/¾ cup) self-raising flour
90 g (3 oz/¾ cup) plain (all-purpose) flour
90 g (3 oz/¾ cup) unsweetened cocoa powder
½ teaspoon bicarbonate of soda (baking soda)
345 g (12 oz/1½ cups) caster (superfine) sugar
3 eggs
1½ tablespoons oil
80 ml (2½ fl oz/⅓ cup) milk
dark, milk and white truffles, to decorate
unsweetened cocoa powder, to sprinkle

Milk chocolate ganache
150 g (5½ oz) milk chocolate chips
125 g (4½ oz) unsalted butter, chopped
60 ml (2 fl oz/¼ cup) whipping cream

Christening cupcakes

MAKES 16

185 g (6½ oz) unsalted butter, softened
170 g (6 oz/¾ cup) caster (superfine) sugar
1 teaspoon natural vanilla extract
3 eggs
125 g (4½ oz/1 cup) self-raising flour
30 g (1 oz/¼ cup) plain (all-purpose) flour
125 ml (4 fl oz/½ cup) milk

Icing (frosting) decoration
500 g (1 lb 2 oz) ready-made white icing
1 egg white, lightly beaten
pink or blue food colouring

Preheat the oven to 180°C (350°F/Gas 4).
Line 16 standard muffin holes with paper cases.

Beat the butter, sugar and vanilla together with electric beaters until light and creamy. Add the eggs, one at a time, beating well after each addition. Sift the flours together and fold in alternately with the milk. Divide the mixture evenly among the cases. Bake for 15 minutes, or until a skewer comes out clean when inserted into the centre of a cake. Transfer onto a wire rack to cool.

To decorate the cakes, roll out 375 g (13 oz) of the white icing, onto a surface dusted with icing sugar, to 5 mm (¼ inch) thick. Using a 7 cm (2¾ inch) scone cutter, cut out 16 rounds. Lightly brush the egg white over each cake and place a round of icing on top.

Add 1 drop of the pink or blue food colouring to the remaining icing and knead until the colouring is well blended. Weigh 32 x 25 g (¼ oz) portions of icing. Roll out each portion into a short sausage shape. Make a bootie by bending the sausage in half. Hollow out the top of the bootie with the rounded end of a small wooden spoon, then thin the edges to make a frill. Lightly brush egg white under each pair of booties and place on top of the cake.

Index

Published in 2008 by Murdoch Books Pty Limited

Murdoch Books Australia
Pier 8/9
23 Hickson Road
Millers Point NSW 2000
Phone: +61 (0) 2 8220 2000
Fax: +61 (0) 2 8220 2558
www.murdochbooks.com.au

Murdoch Books UK Limited
Erico House, 6th Floor
93–99 Upper Richmond Road
Putney, London SW15 2TG
Phone: +44 (0) 20 8785 5995
Fax: +44 (0) 20 8785 5985
www.murdochbooks.co.uk

Chief Executive: Juliet Rogers
Publishing Director: Kay Scarlett

Commissioning editor: Jane Lawson
Editor: Sandra Davies
Food editor: Chrissy Freer
Design Concept: Reuben Crossman
Design layout: Melanie Ngapo
Photographer: Brett Stevens
Stylist: Lynsey Fryers
Food preparation: Peta Dent
Recipes by: Lee Currie and the Murdoch Books test kitchen
Production: Nikla Martin

National Library of Australia Cataloguing-in-Publication Data
Indulgence cookies / editor, Sandra Davies.
ISBN: 978 1 7419 6120 1 (hbk.)
Series: Indulgence series. Includes index.
1. Cupcakes. 641.8653

A catalogue record for this book is available from the
British Library.

Colour separation by COLOUR CHIEFS PTY LTD

Printed by 1010 Printing International Limited in 2008.
PRINTED IN CHINA. Reprinted 2009 (twice).

The Publisher and stylist would like to thank Anibou,
Australian Salvage Company, Crowley & Grouch, Domayne
Design, Empire Homewares, Koskela, Miljo, Mokum Textiles
and Tres Fabu! for lending equipment for use and
photography.

IMPORTANT: Those who might be at risk from the effects of
salmonella poisoning (the elderly, pregnant women, young
children and those suffering from immune deficiency
diseases) should consult their doctor with any concerns about
eating raw eggs.

OVEN GUIDE: You may find cooking times vary depending
on the oven you are using. For fan-forced ovens, as a general
rule, set the oven temperature to 20°C (35°F) lower than
indicated in the recipe.